ARTIST ARCHIVES™ INTRODUCTION BY MAX ALLAN COLLINS

INDIAN MAIDENS

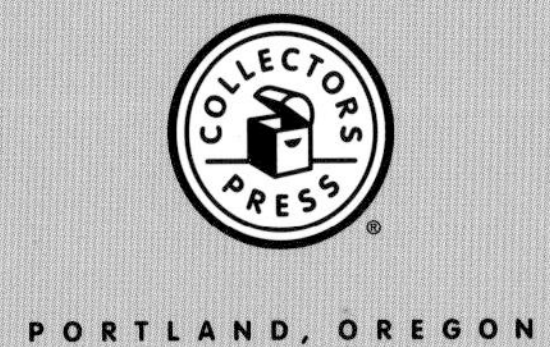

PORTLAND, OREGON

INTRODUCTION

Art Direction Principia Graphica
Design Hoover H.Y. Li
Editor Lori Stephens

The artwork contained herein is from the archives of Collectors Press, Inc. We are always seeking to expand our collection. If you are interested in selling your pin-up originals or ephemera please contact Collectors Press, Inc.

Printed in China

Library of Congress Cataloging-in-Publication Data
Collins, Max Allan.
Indian maidens / Max Allan Collins. — 1st American ed.
p. cm. — (Artist archives)
ISBN 1-888054-46-8
1. Commercial art – United States – History – 20th century 2.Women in art . 3.Indians in popular culture – United States. I. Title. II. Series.
NC998.5.A1 C65 2001
00-012696
CIP

First American Edition

9 8 7 6 5 4 3 2 1

FOR A FREE CATALOG WRITE TO COLLECTORS PRESS, INC.

P.O. Box 230986
Portland, Oregon 97281
Toll Free 800-423-1848
Or visit our website at *www.collectorspress.com*

TRYING TO IDENTIFY the exact tribes to which the Indian maids in this volume belong would be a pointless exercise. The term "Native American" (rejected by many American Indians, by the way) was to come in the distant future, whereas the calendar artists represented here attempted to invoke a recent past. That takes nothing away from the naive charm and adept artistry displayed in these pages. The Old West has fed vivid images into popular culture from the very beginning, when hack writer Ned Buntline fashioned Dime Novels from the exploits of real cowboys and lawmen and Buffalo Bill Cody took his Wild West show on the road. Whether it's Roy Rogers or Gene Autry singing from a saddle, or John Wayne blowing away bad guys in John Ford and Howard Hawks films, the pop culture phenomenon known as "Cowboys and Indians" has never had much to do with the real thing. Check out photographs of actual western saloons and match them to the Hollywood honky-tonk images in your mind; compare the real Wyatt Earp to the various actors who have portrayed him.

While these images of beautiful Indian maidens have nothing to do with reality, they have everything to do with romantic fantasy. In their wonderful book *Vintage Illustration* (Collectors Press, 1997), authors Rick and Charlotte Martin say Indian maiden images "represent a last gasp at romanticizing the closing of the Old West at the end of the nineteenth century." True enough, but these images also represent what Broadway showman Florenz Ziegfeld termed "Glorifying the American Girl." And for all their headbands, beads, braids, fringed buckskin, and colorful feathers, these are typical, clearly Caucasian girls-next-door posed in exotic settings, the use of which seems to justify, even validate, the depiction of young, pulchritudinous lasses in skimpy attire.

None of the artists represented here bothered to spend much, if any time, researching Indian culture, and their chief inspiration was most likely the Broadway showgirls of the aforementioned Ziegfeld. And the idealized outdoor settings of these prints had much more to do with Maxfield Parrish than Frederic Remington.

Though most of the images here date to the 1920s and early 1930s, the idealized Americanized Indian maid image was a popular advertising image from 1910 until the early 1940s when more provocative pin-ups with contemporary settings became the standard. In the window between the two world wars, however, Indian maids could be seen (among other places) on cigar boxes, sheet music, almanac covers, blotters and, of course, calendars. Even in the 1950s, the idealized Indian maiden lingered: witness the Tiger Lily of Disney's and Mary Martin's Peter Pan and Howdy Doody's Princess Summerfallwinterspring.

If Florenz Ziegfeld and his vision of glamour impacted on the painters herein, those painters influenced the great showman himself. Ziegfeld's showgirls were a staple of his elaborate musical stage revues, and the Indian princesses came along for the ride when one of his rare "book" musicals was brought to the screen in 1930: the Eddie Cantor sensation, "Whoopee!" Largely forgotten today, bouncy "banjo-eyed" singer/comedian Cantor was a superstar of the first half of the twentieth century, and "Whoopee!" was perhaps his most successful vehicle. Available on home video and occasionally seen on cable television, "Whoopee!" sports extravagant costumes, Charleston-style dancing, and dated humor that make it a snapshot of the 1920s. Like Al Jolson, the energetic, often very funny Cantor made his mark on Broadway working in black face, and "Whoopee!" contains one of those trademark routines. Combined with depictions of Indians in a musical comedy, set in the American West desert, these elements make the early "talkie" a virtual fest of political incorrectness.

Shot in surreal two-strip Technicolor, featuring Busby Berkley's first choreography in a motion picture, "Whoopee!" prominently features Ziegfeld's showgirls (co-opted by the film's producer into Goldwyn Girls). The girls are particularly highlighted in a finale in which one Indian maiden after another (including young future superstar Betty Grable) parades down a ramp in lavish yet skimpy costumes, often with elaborate feather headdresses, occasionally riding a pony. In a motion picture that was a huge smash in its day and now considered a campy classic, this sequence is a virtual calendar come to life, clearly intended to invoke the popular images seen in these pages. It is proof positive that the idealized image of the regal Indian princess held enormous popular appeal in an era we associate with zany Clara Bow-esque flappers.

Some of the artists here are unknown, and at least a few of these images are as yet unidentified. Several artists responsible for Indian maid prints were minor figures in American illustration (R. Atkinson Fox and Edward Mason Eggleston, for instance). Whether star performer or anonymous artisan, the painters shared a common approach. The maiden was decidedly non-ethnic in appearance; her attire was not always overtly skimpy, but her arms and legs (at least) were bare. Nymph of nature that she was, a maiden might occasionally appear sans anything but, say, a headdress. The backgrounds were inevitably elaborate, in part because most of these artists were landscape painters, but also to establish settings that invoked wild nature.

A typical example is the image "Indian Love Call." Her wistful stare, beads, and long braids are typical, as are her bare shoulders and lovely legs, right down to her toes. Artist Homer Nelson crammed so much landscape into his painting that he might have overwhelmed his central subject had she not been so lovely. What is perhaps unusual in Nelson's maid is a sense of melancholy; a theme of loss — loss of innocence or of the wilderness — that might be expected to turn up frequently in this genre but rarely does.

Like many of America's best illustrators, Homer Nelson was a student at the Art Institute of Chicago. He also studied in Denver, Colorado, and traveled extensively in the southwest, making Nelson the rare "Indian maidens" painter who may have actually researched his subject. In his series "Indian Heroines," his portrayal of artifacts and apparel hews closer to reality than most of the genre, but such is faint praise. Better to extol his vivid color sense and his elaborate nature backgrounds.

The maidens of F.R. Harper (1876-1948) have much in common with Nelson's "Indian Love Call." They, too, perch fetchingly near a stream, staring wistfully, and Harper's backgrounds are elaborate and similarly packed with detail and scenic quality. But Harper's girls (and they are girls, not women) lack any sense of melancholy; their fringed dresses are so far off the shoulder as to nearly expose a suspiciously pale breast or two. Proud of her lipsticked prettiness, the lass by the waterfall has moved overtly into the pin-up area. A native of Rock Island, Illinois, Harper also studied at the Art Institute of Chicago, that wellspring of American calendar artists. Harper had a career outside of advertising as a fine artist, and his works were shown in the Metropolitan Museum in New York. Still, he survived by taking on commercial accounts, and Harper specialized in historical and patriotic subjects, as well as "pretty girls."

Charles M. Reylea (1863-1932) puts somewhat less emphasis on the backgrounds of his Indian maiden paintings than is the norm for the genre. His untitled painting in which a maiden perched on a red blanket on a cliff studies the moonlight, with the rocky landscape (complete with waterfall) gives us a much closer look than usual at its pretty subject. This maiden seems young and contemporary, in a flapper sense, as do the preening princesses in the other Reylea example, one seated in a canoe, the other on an island shore. These are girls going to a masquerade as Indian maids or maybe to the prom.

Particularly in the latter painting of the two princesses, Reylea displays an indifference to the background, barely stroking it in, but lavishes love and detailed work on his beautiful subjects. Born in Albany, New York, during the Civil War, Reylea attended the Pennsylvania Academy of Fine Arts, where he studied with Thomas Eakins in the late 1880s. He continued his schooling in Paris and wound up back in New York, where he contributed illustrations to such prominent magazines as *Century* and *St. Nicholas*. He excelled in the calendar field, however, and over a dozen Indian maiden calendars are attributed to him.

R. Atkinson Fox (1860-1935) is represented herein by the wonderful "Daughter of the Rising Sun," a painting which appeared the year that "Whoopee!" opened on Broadway (1928). It's hard to know who was mimicking whom — Fox or Ziegfeld — as "Daughter" makes no pretense at accuracy. Its graceful, dancing, impossibly beautiful Indian princess is, right down to the lipstick and cheek rouge, a Broadway showgirl. If we find the headdress and beaded bikini a masterpiece of camp from our end of the telescope, we should not ignore the simple majesty of the composition or the elegance and relative restraint of the Parrish-like landscape before which Fox's showgirl struts her stuff.

Born in Toronto, Ontario, Canada, Fox studied at the Ontario Society for Artists, traveling extensively and sporadically studying in Europe. Initially a respected portrait painter, Fox lived in several East Coast cities until moving to Chicago to be near a major client. He contributed at least 1,000 prints to clients including calendar publishers, picture-framing companies, and printers. So prolific was he and so in demand that he worked in countless genres and under numerous pen names.

Once dismissed as a second-string Maxfield Parrish (and derided for his many bucolic scenes featuring cows!) Fox's stature has grown in recent years, as collectors have become interested in his uniquely American meld of realism and romanticism. Some of his paintings might be dismissed as dull, but his "Daughter of the Setting Sun" is arguably the most beautiful in this book.

Or should that honor go to Edward Mason Eggleston's "Flaming Arrow"?

Eggleston's untitled painting depicts two Indian sisters perched cliffside, one standing, one seated, both peering anxiously toward an off-camera horizon against a Parrish-like landscape. Eggleston proved that he could serve up typical, lovely slices of the Indian maiden genre.

Born in Ashtabula, Ohio, Eggleston (1887-1941) studied at the Columbus Art School, and his distinguished teachers included Harvey Dunn, an acolyte of Howard Pyle, top illustrator of his day. Working out of New York, Eggleston made his mark in commercial illustration, creating the famous image of the sleepy child lugging a tire and a candle ("Time to Retire") for the Fisk Tire Company.

In "Flaming Arrow," perhaps the latest of our images (1934), Eggleston leaves behind any lingering traces of Art Nouveau and moves boldly into starkly Art Deco design and execution. All that is left of Maxfield Parrish are the vivid shades of blue and the bold presence of orange in the maid's stunningly detailed headdress. Uncluttered and striking, "Flaming Arrow" presents a princess who in her near nudity manages to be an unabashed pin-up girl even as she exudes a regal bearing worthy of any Indian princess.

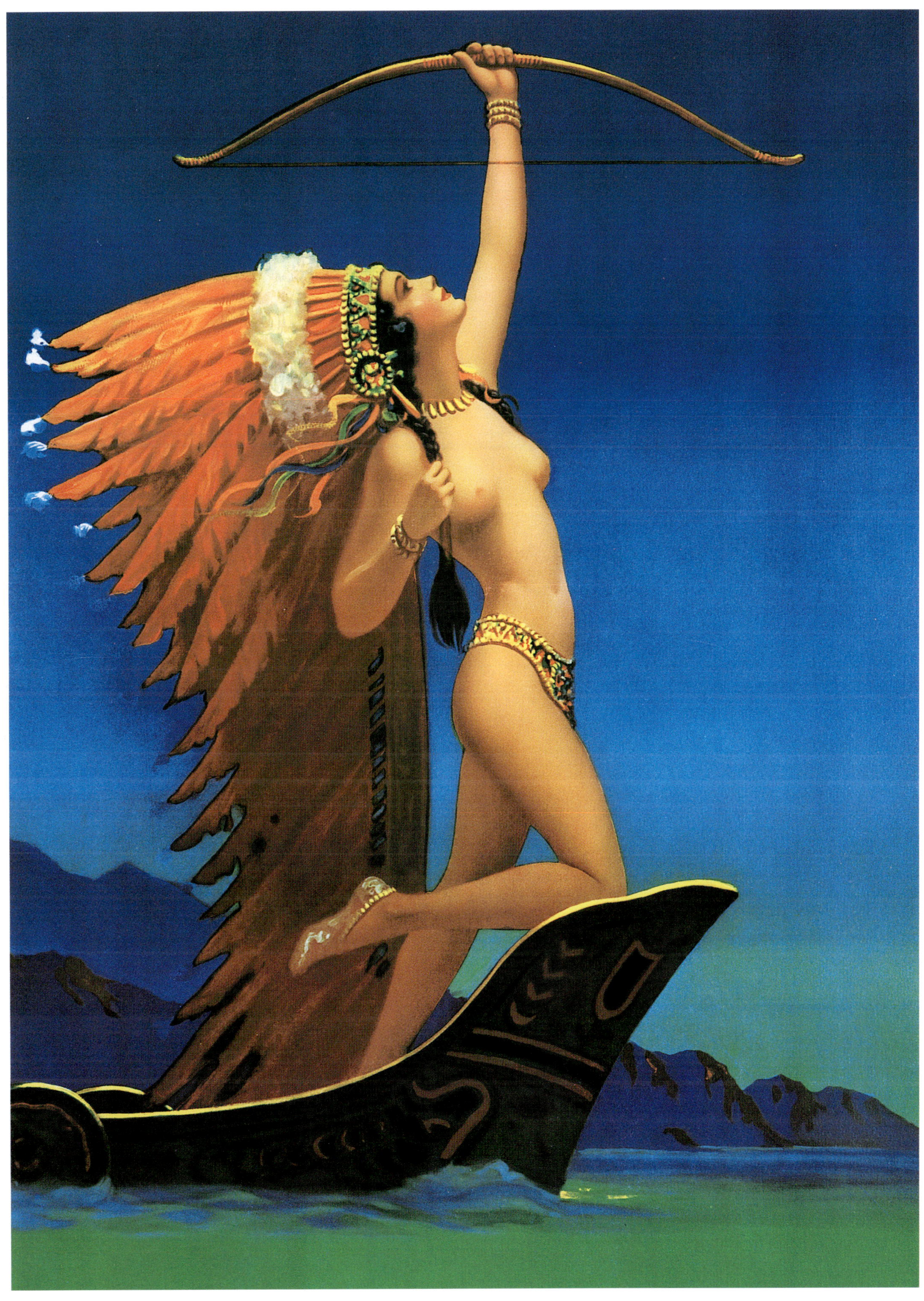

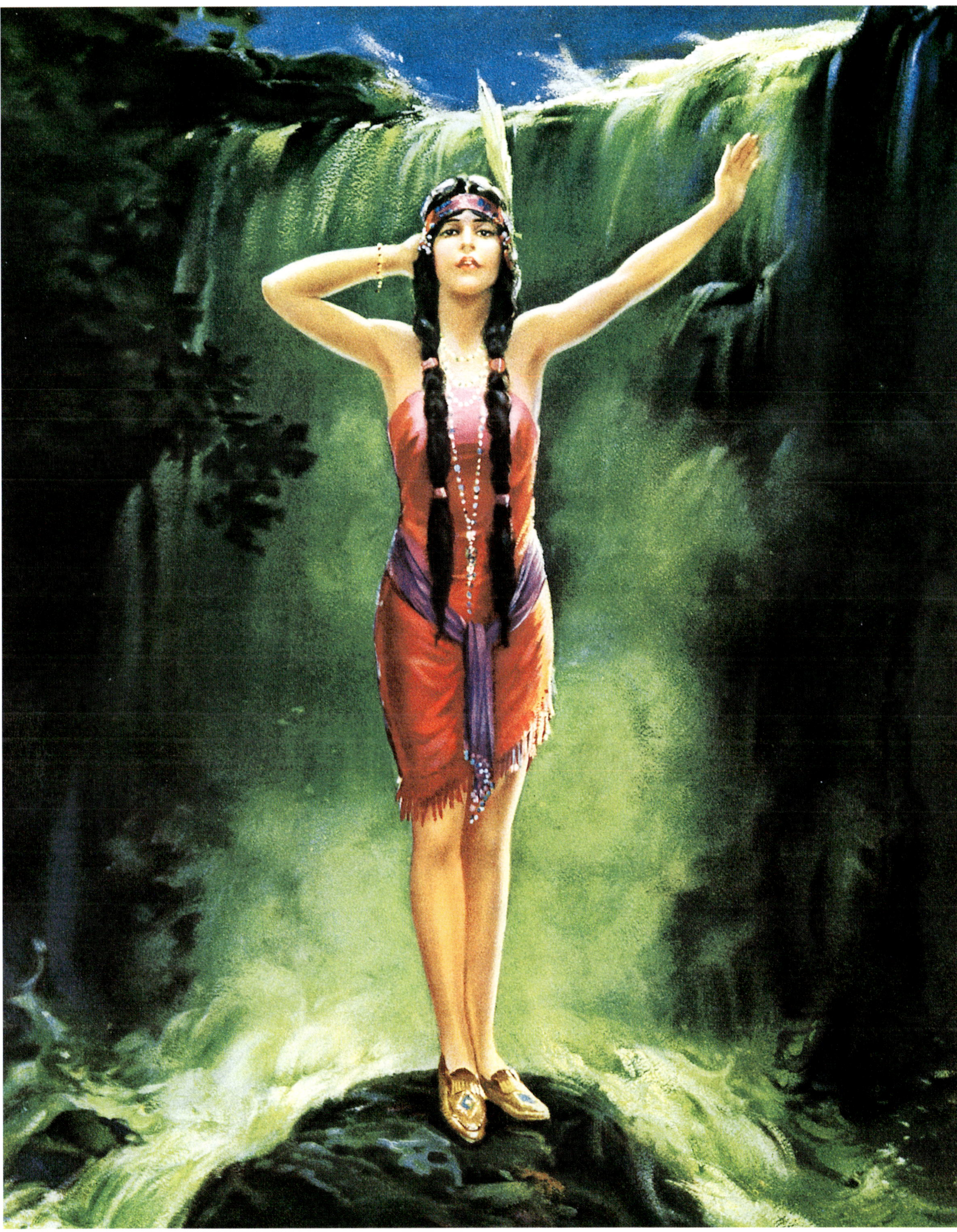

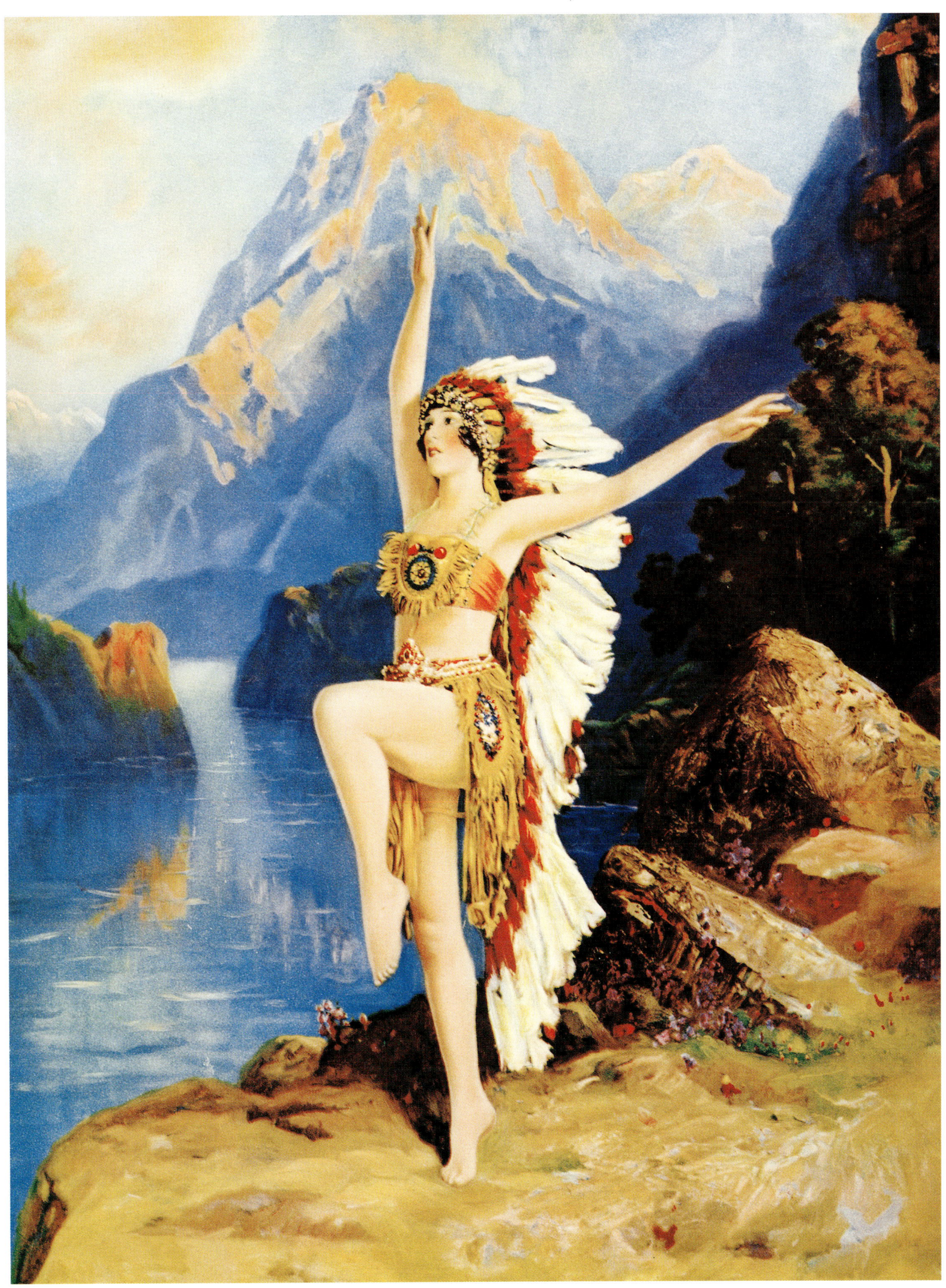

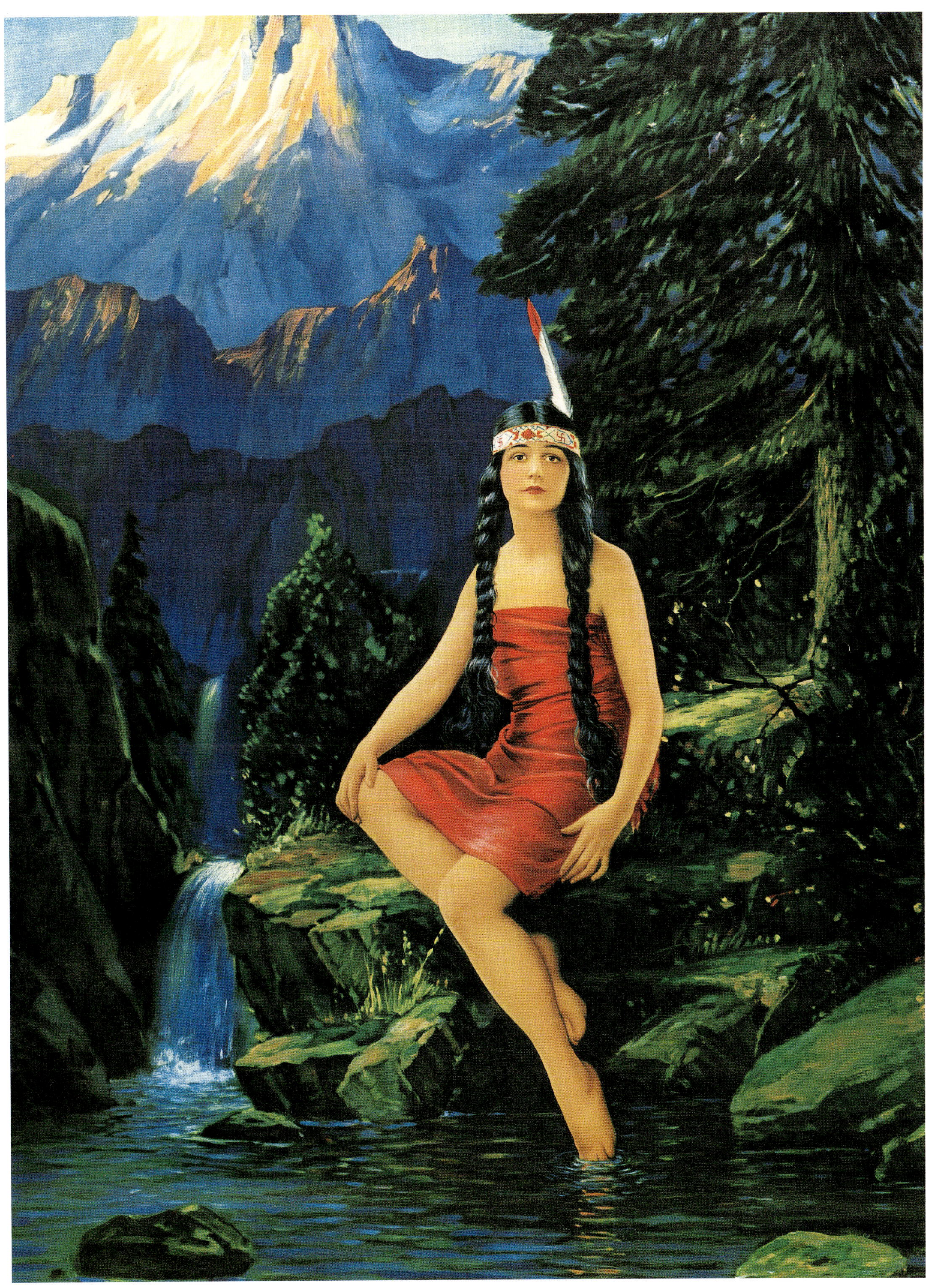

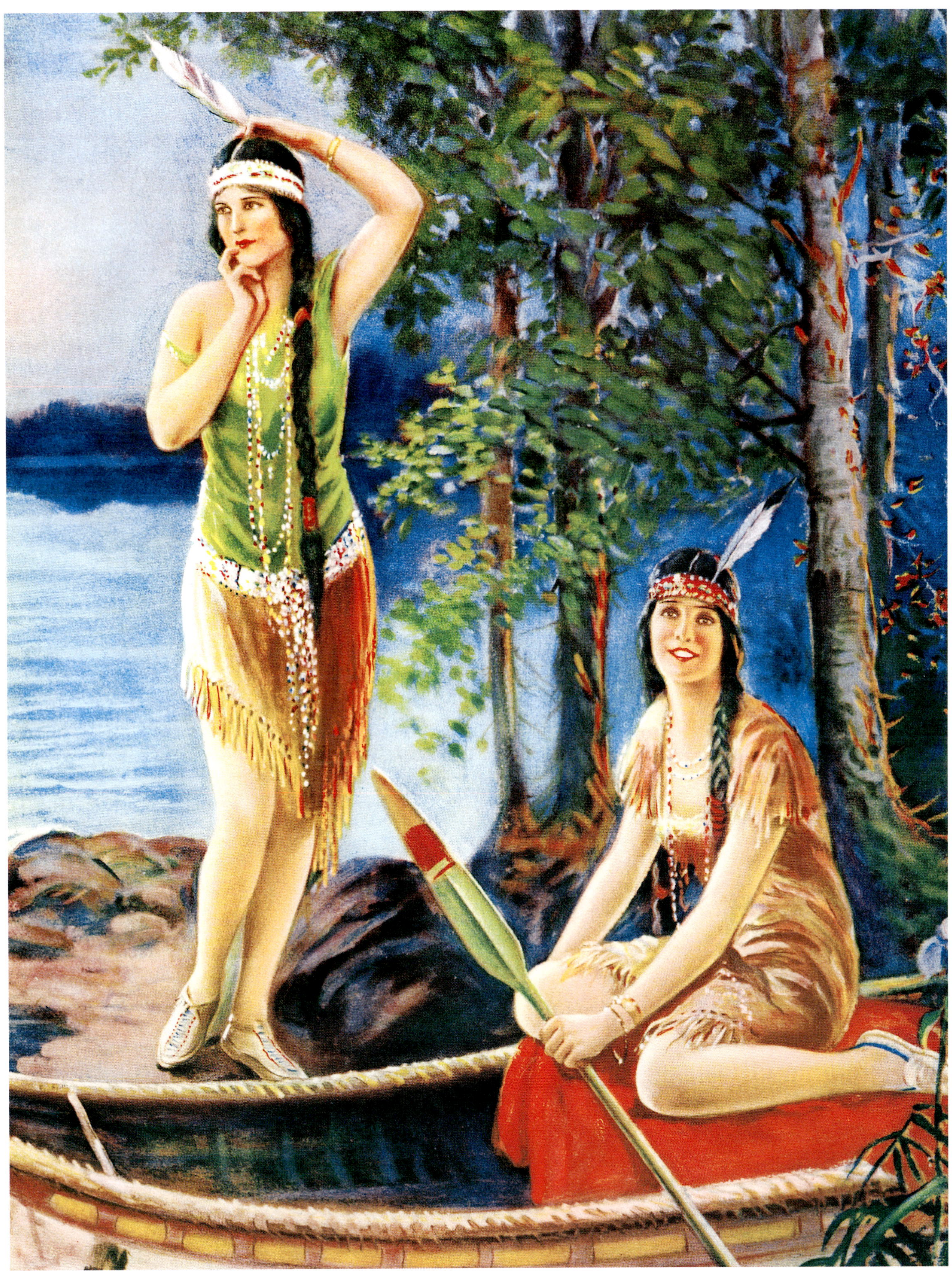

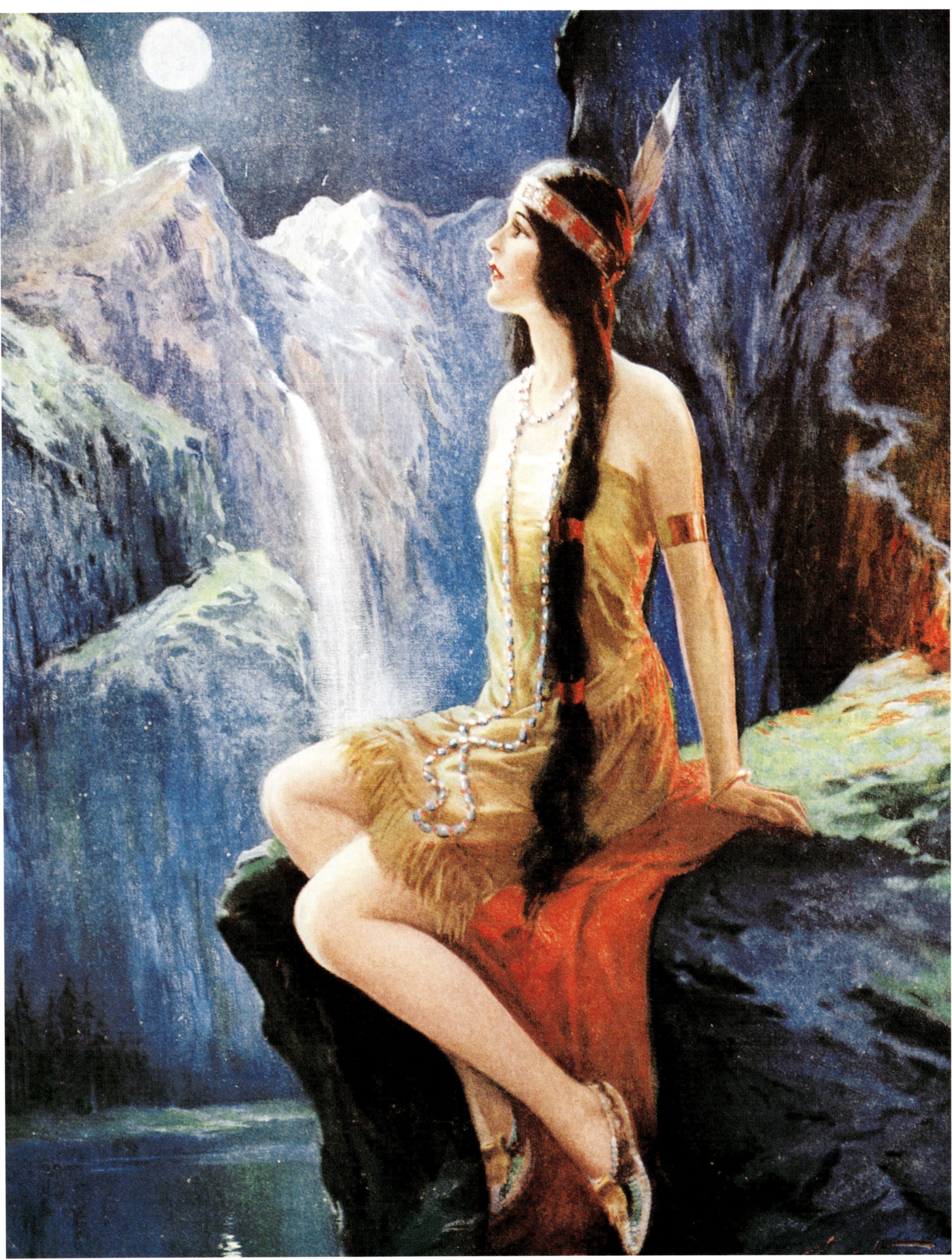

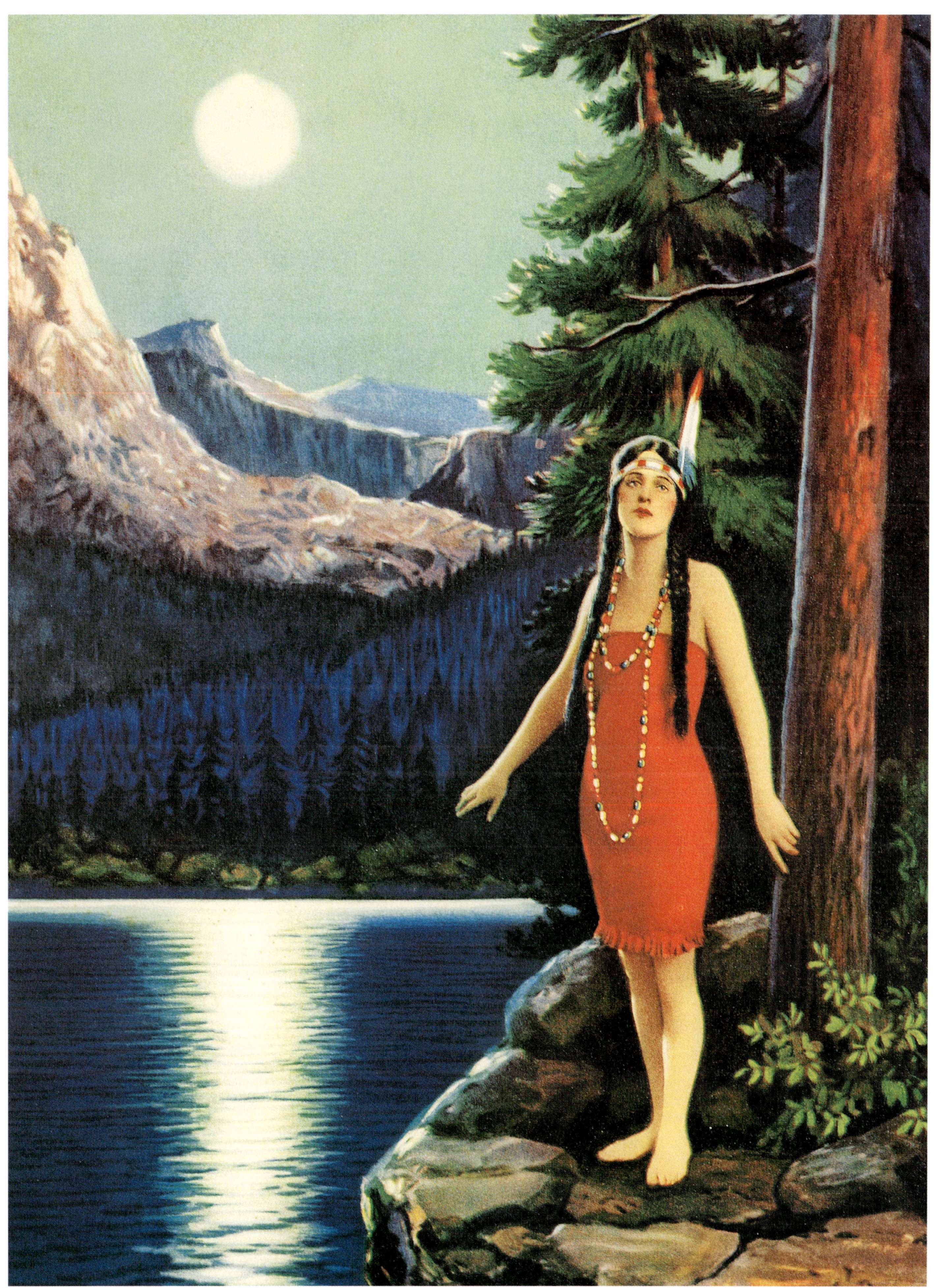

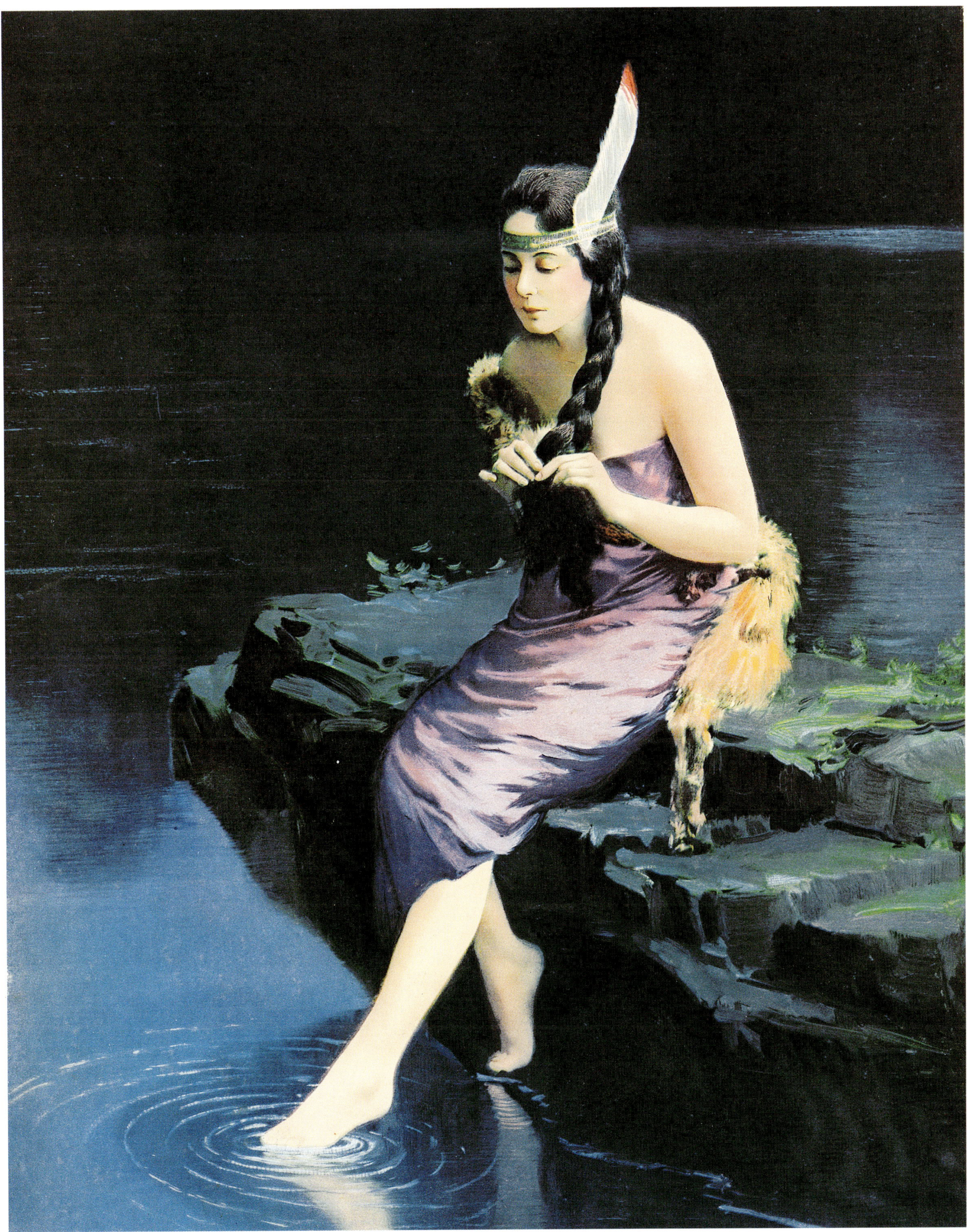

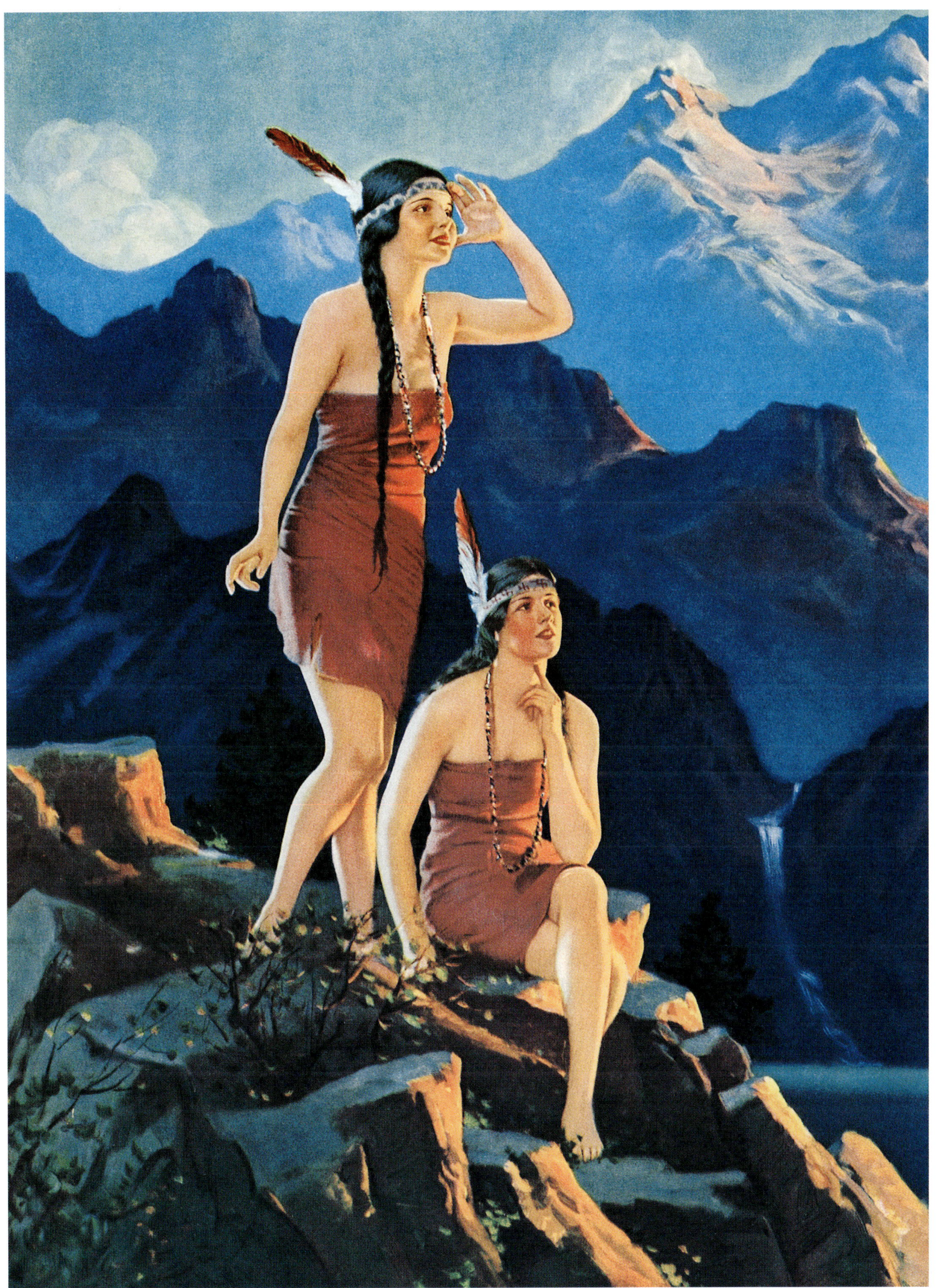

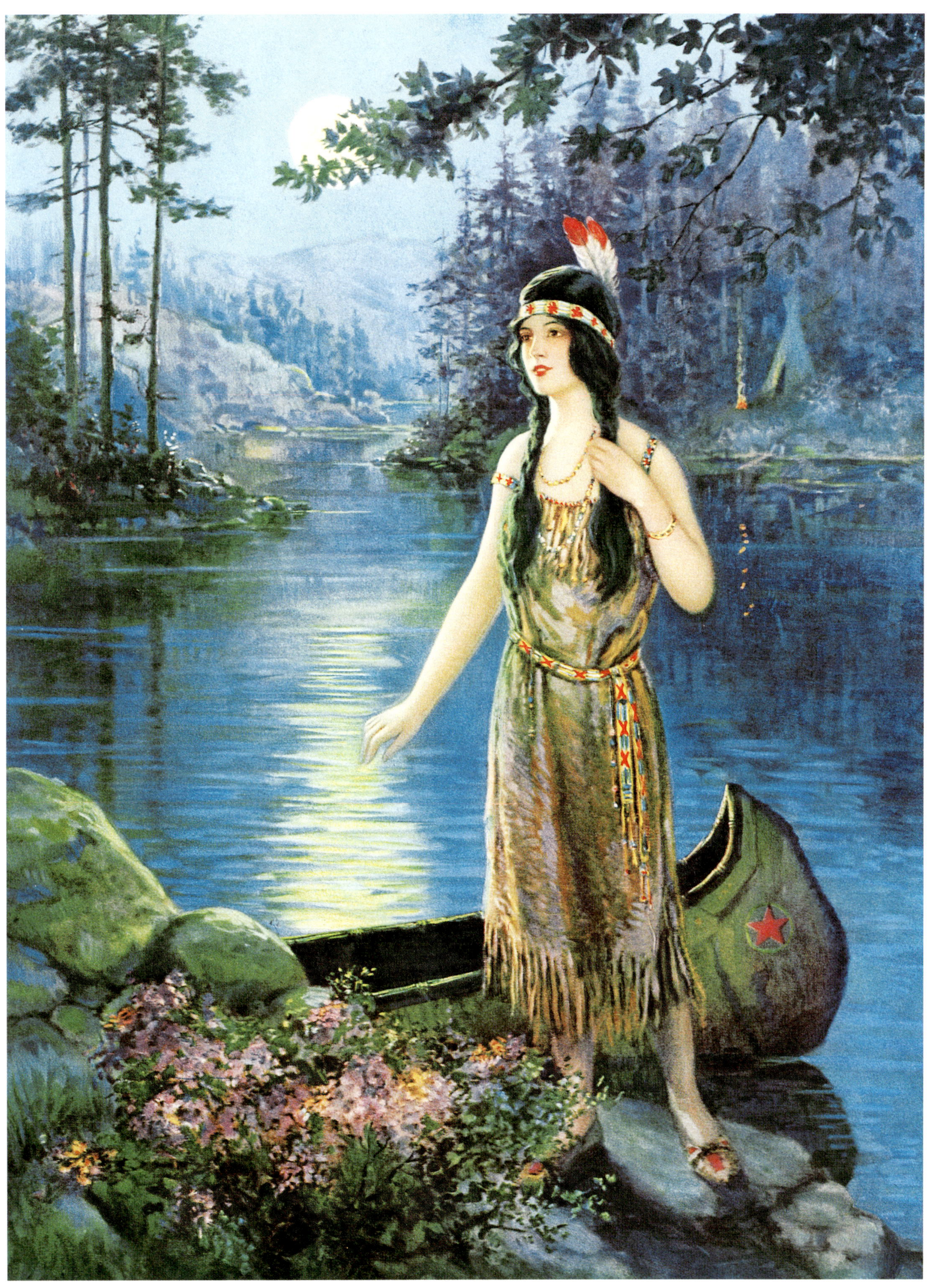

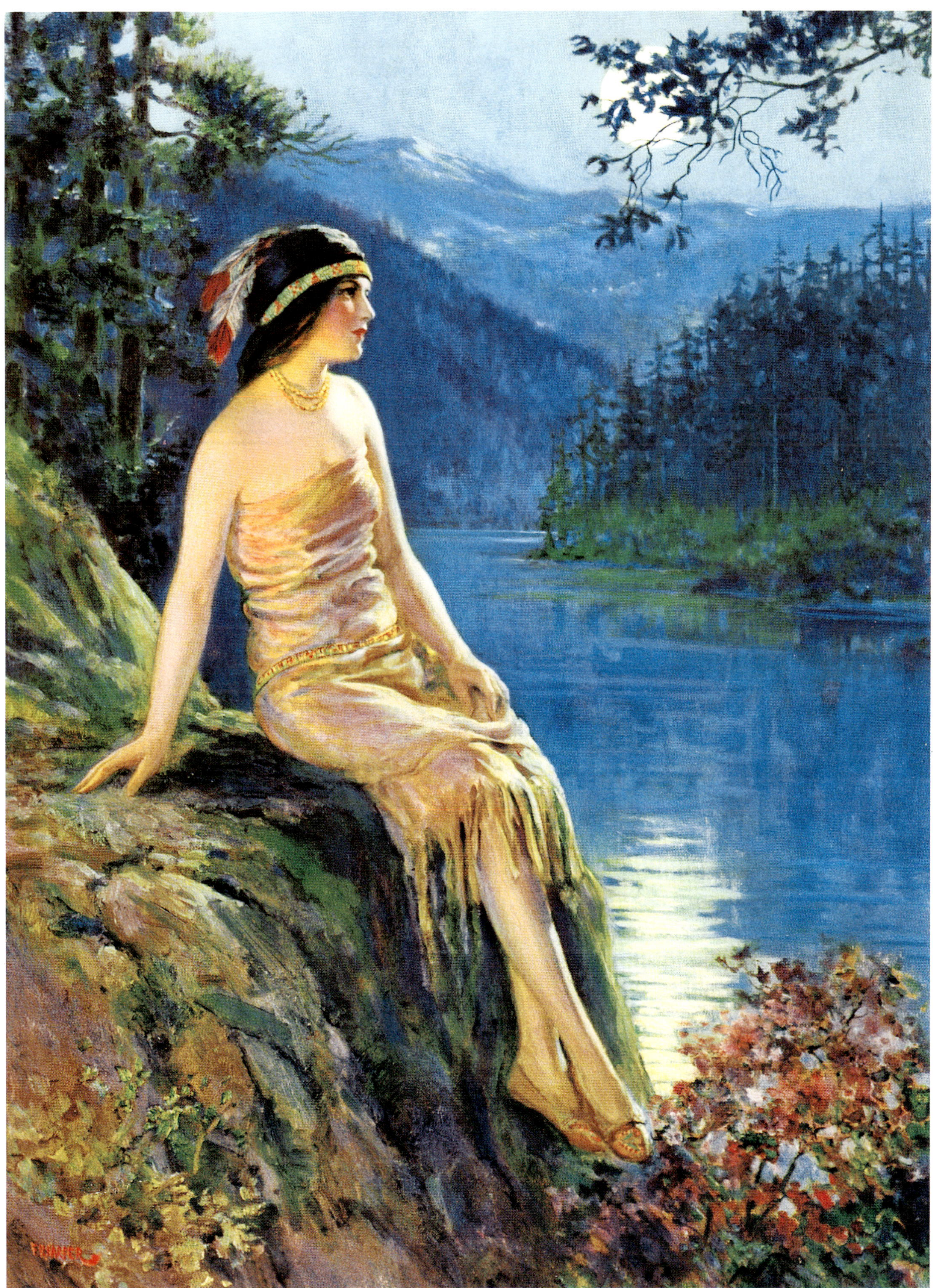

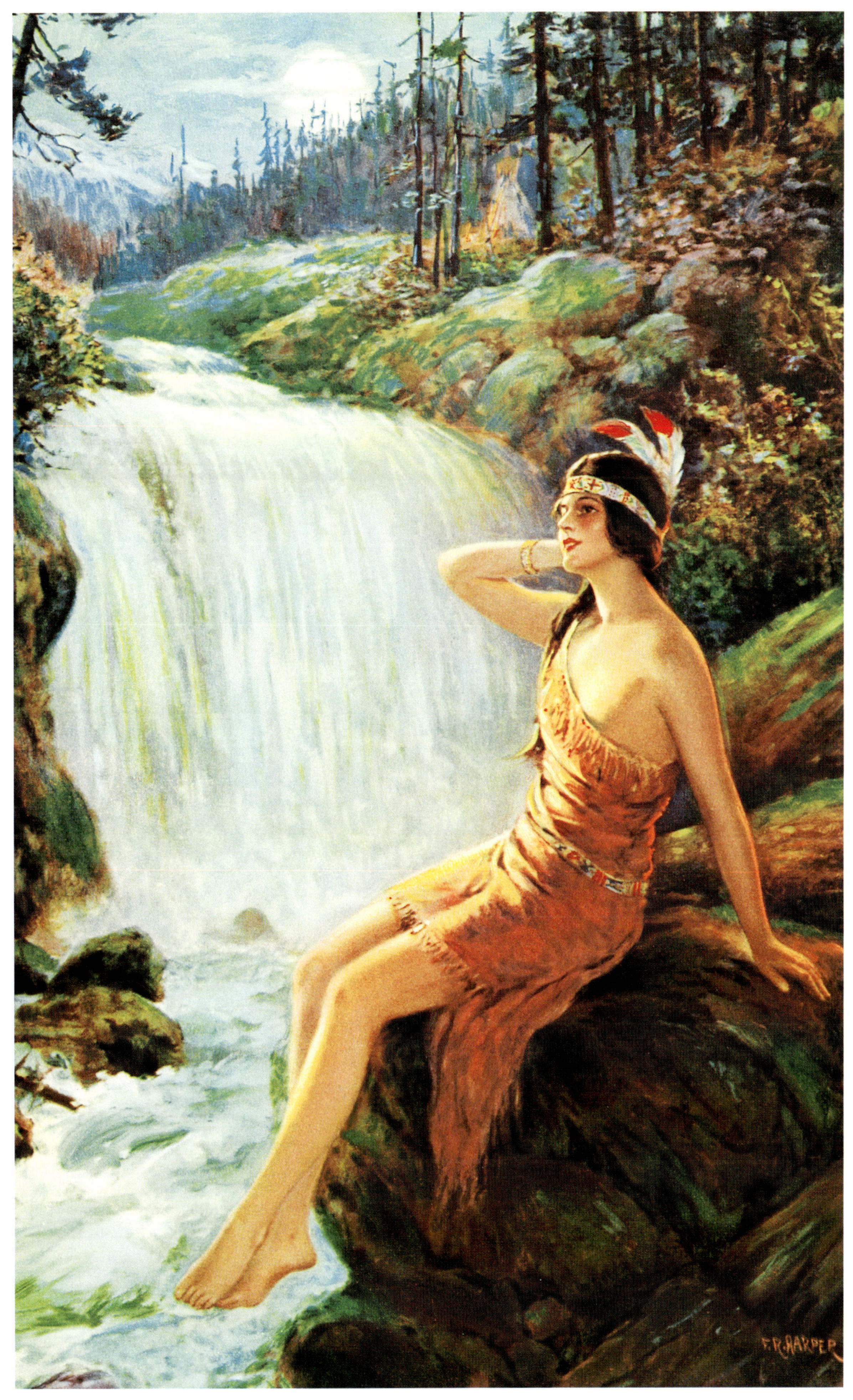
F.R. HARPER

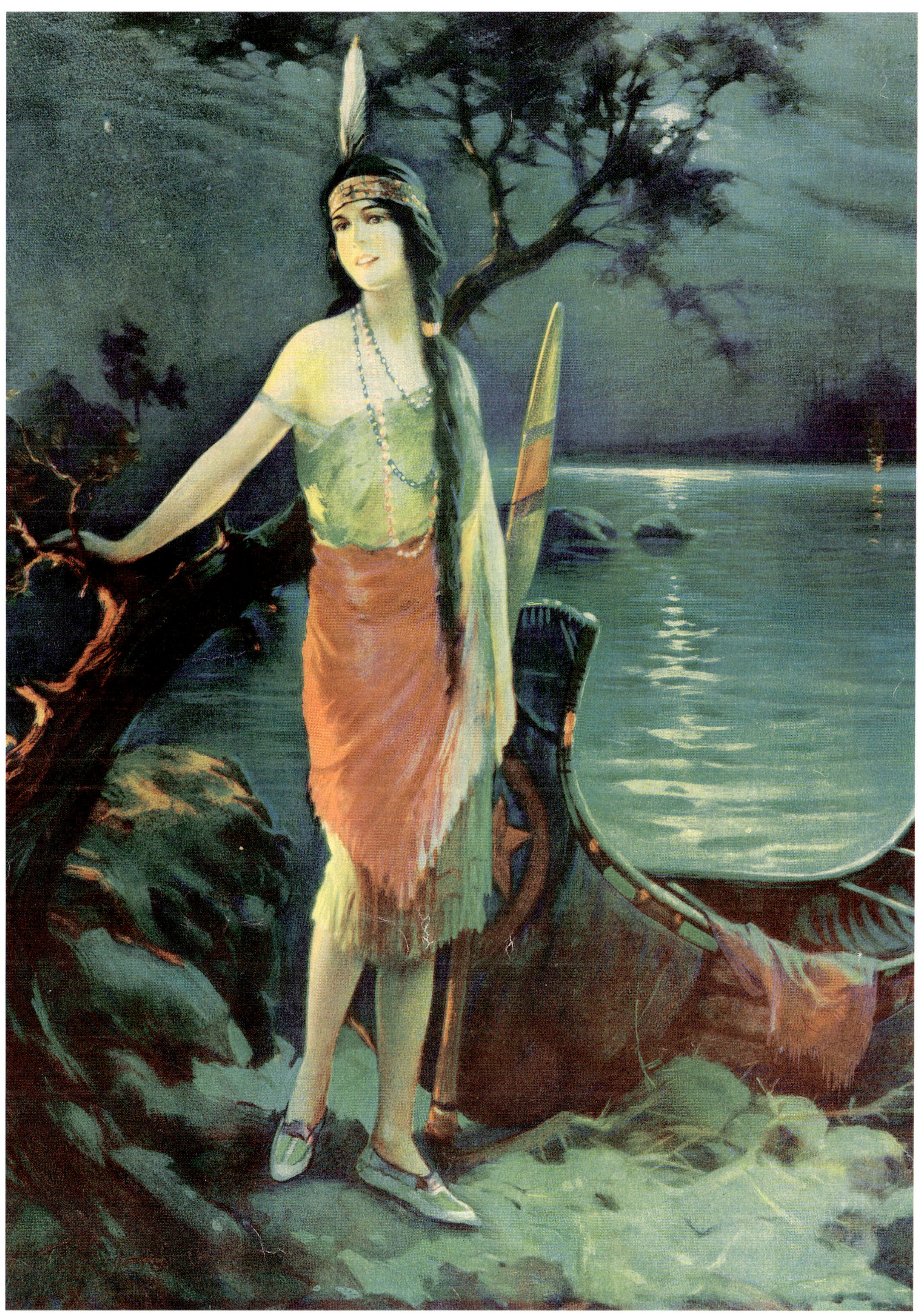

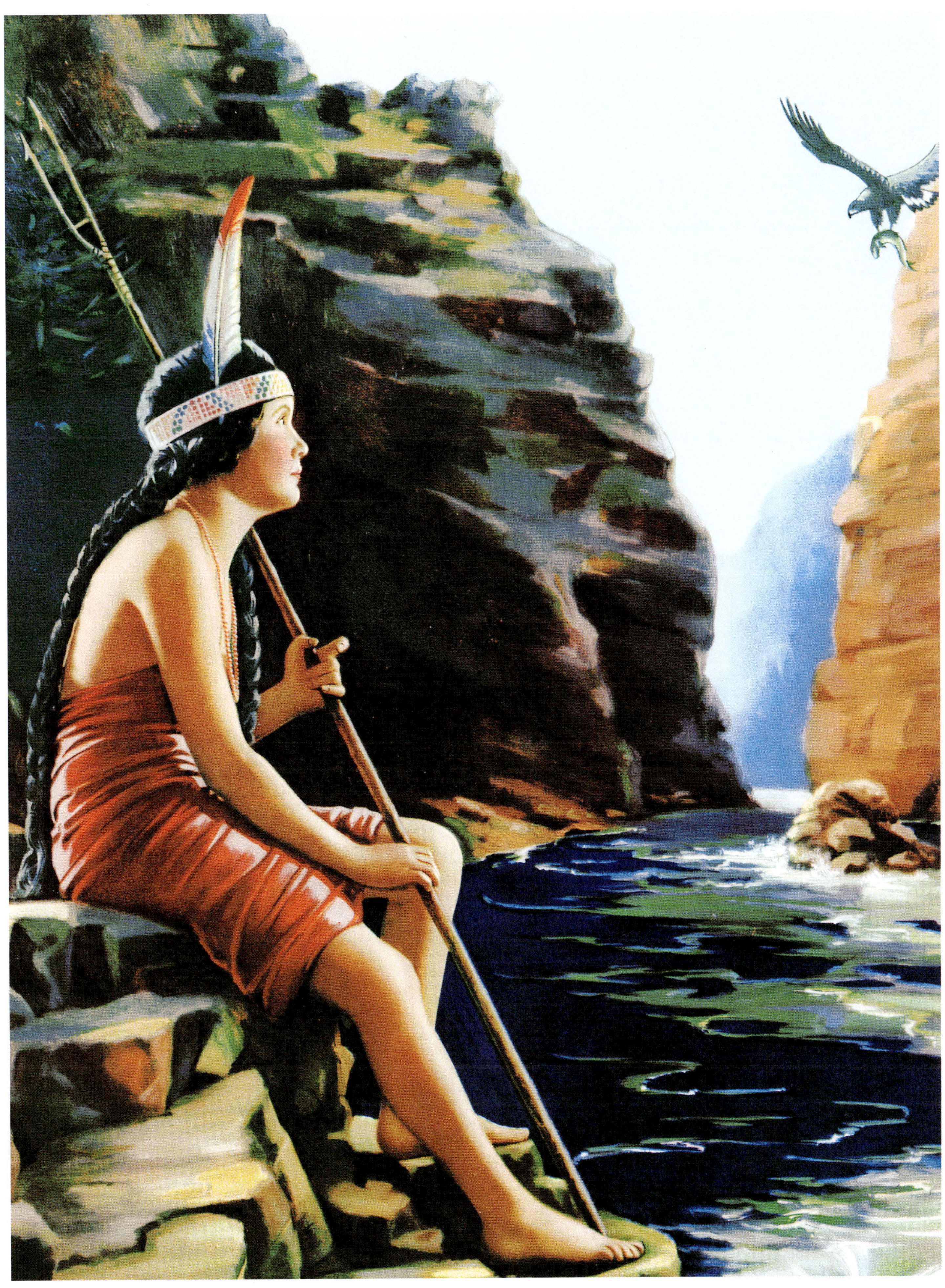